INVESTING IN YOUR SUCCESS

A Practical Guide to Achieving Your Best Results in Your First Year of Law School

Kia H. Vernon and Krishnee G. Coley

Investing in Your Success

A Practical Guide to Achieving Your Best Results in Your First Year of Law School

Investing in Your Success

A Practical Guide to Achieving Your Best Results in Your First Year of Law School

Kia H. Vernon

Assistant Professor
North Carolina Central University School of Law

Krishnee G. Coley

Director of Academic Support
North Carolina Central University School of Law

Continuing Education Center of North Carolina, LLC

Continuing Education Center of North Carolina, LLC
301 Kilmayne Drive, Suite 203
Cary, North Carolina 27511
Email: cecnc@mail.com

Table of Contents

ACKNOWLEDGMENTS

To my mom, Johnsie Gaddy, and my brother and sister, Jas' and Kenaysha, thank you for always supporting me and encouraging me to do my best; to my husband, Charles and my children, Raya and Jaden, thank you for your love and support and for eating take-out on all the nights I had to work on the book.

-KC

To my parents, Bob and Mary Hardy and my brother Bobby, thank you for your encouragement in all my endeavors; to my husband Kurt, thank you for constantly telling me to "gussy-up" and to my children, Mia, Kori and Kara, thank you for being my inspirations and my reasons for being.

-KV

To our research assistant, Shanai Harris, thank you for your diligence and insightful critiques; to Professor Pamela Newell, thank you for taking the time to review our work and for assisting us with your expertise in legal writing; and to North Carolina Central University School of Law, thank you for your part in our successes and for allowing us to teach and inspire.

-KC and KV

ABOUT THIS BOOK

This book was written for students interested in, planning to attend, or currently enrolled in their first year of law school. As you probably have discovered, there are numerous books targeted for this group which seek to advise students on how to do well in law school. What sets this book apart is its conversational tone and its narrowly tailored focus, which makes the information easier to understand and addresses the specific issues that students have difficulty with in their first year.

This book was conceived after the two of us, who attended law school together without having the benefit of knowing what to expect or what would enable us to receive the best results in law school, found ourselves over a decade later back in law school–this time teaching and advising students. We discovered that students were still misinformed or simply uninformed about the realities of law school. Consequently, we started this book to provide students with facts and guidance based on our years attending law school and our years working in law school.

Since our experiences and viewpoints (then and now) are so similar we chose to write this book in first person and as one voice instead of two. This gives the book an informal feel and makes it an "easy read" for students. This book is organized and written with the intention that once you start reading it, you will continue reading it until you have read the last page. This book is full of valuable information that would have benefitted us tremendously if we had access to it when we were embarking on our journeys in law school. You will only achieve the most benefit if you read it all.

On a final note, although it hasn't been that long since we have been in law school, this book was written from our prospective as professors. While we try to remain objective, since we are professors, we offer advice which supports the institution and value of the law school process and discourages students from taking shortcuts and trying to find the easy way to get through the first year. It is not our intention that you just "get through" the first year of law school, but that you do well in your first year and beyond.

"Decide that you want it more than you are afraid of it."

-Bill Cosby

INTRODUCTIONS

I wish there was a book like this when I was about to enter law school. At the time, I was clueless. I made the decision to go to law school for all the wrong reasons: I think I read too much Grisham; I changed my mind about medical school; and since I was not ready to be a grown-up and enter the workforce, I applied to law school. While it is hard to believe and I would not recommend this for you, I was accepted and entered law school without ever setting foot on the campus that I was going to give all my time and money to for the next three years. I remember feeling overwhelmed during Orientation and ready to run out the door.

Looking back at the young and naive twenty-two year old I was then, I realize that I had not prepared myself for the rigors of law school. Quickly, I learned that being "smart" and making good grades in college was the baseline where we all started in law school. Thankfully, I am a fast learner and channeled my fear into motivation to do my best. I checked my ego at the door and sought help wherever I could find it. I read and briefed every case, regularly attended classes, joined a study group (even though I didn't realize at the time why I needed to be in one), outlined, studied flash cards and took practice tests. I did it all because that is what I was told to do and I was too stubborn to fail.

Now, I am back at law school less than a decade later, and I see the same look of fear and confusion on the students' faces that was on my face when I started. Law school is still difficult and one of the most challenging educational experiences that you can go through. Ultimately, I hope this book will do a little to lessen the fear and get you ready to succeed in law school.

-KC

"There are no shortcuts to anyplace worth going."

-Beverly Sills

"We're not in Kansas anymore, Toto." This quote reminds me of my first week in law school, when I found myself wondering why I ever decided to go to law school. After only a few days in this new world, it was apparent to me that law school was nothing like I imagined it would be. As a top graduate in my high school, an honors graduate from college and a high-school teacher for four years, I was accustomed to getting good grades and working hard. I did not expect law school to be easy, but I did not expect it to be that arduous either. I was prepared to apply the same work ethic and formula I applied in prior academic endeavors, but I soon realized that studying was simply not enough. I spent many days and nights questioning whether I made the right decision in choosing to end my teaching career and pursue my dream of being a lawyer.

As the first semester progressed, the second guessing continued. Despite spending every spare second of my free time studying, briefing cases and making outlines, I was becoming increasingly worried that I would not be able to maintain the grade point average required to maintain my scholarship. My fiancé at the time, who was no stranger to the rigor and demands of completing a graduate program—having completed medical school, residency, an internship in Internal Medicine and a fellowship in Gastroenterology—could not fathom how difficult law school was. I remember several instances when I was in tears and in a state of near hysteria over the tremendous amount of stress I was under. My fiancé, a consummate learner (or as I affectionately call him, a "geek"), had briefly considered attending law school. He quickly changed his mind after he witnessed how difficult it was.

Now, over ten years later, I can look back on that first year with amusement. Although I can still remember the demanding process of law school as if it were yesterday, I no longer view it in the same manner as I did while I was there. There really is a point to it all. The experience, what I equate to academic hazing, taught me a great deal about the law, and most importantly about myself.

This book is intended to prepare rising first year law school students for their new life in law school. The purpose of this book is to provide you with a glance into law school: what to expect, how to effectively manage your time, how to prepare for classes, how and what to study, how to prepare for and approach law school exams and where to go for assistance in law school. It is my hope that the pages that follow will provide you with a realistic look at law school, as well as provide helpful information that, if applied, will assist you in achieving your best results your first year in law school.

I am living proof that it can be done. I not only graduated from law school, I graduated with honors. I know this sounds so cliché, but if I can do it, I know that you can too. I wish you all the best in your new endeavor. Now... let's get started!

-KV

"Success is a journey, not a destination."

-Ben Sweetland

Chapter 1

Preparing Yourself for Law School

Welcome to Law School

Congratulations! You have just been accepted to law school and are about to begin your legal studies. Whether you are a recent college graduate, changing careers or a "professional" student, there a number of secrets to succeeding in law school that I want to share with you. Most people find law school to be more challenging than college. What worked for you prior to law school may not be as helpful as you maneuver through the murky and treacherous waters of a legal education.

The New Faces of Law School

The faces of law school are changing. Long gone are the days when the graduating law school class picture resembled a picture from a college men's rowing team. Law schools today reflect the diversity of our country. But the heterogeneity exists not only in the gender and ethnicity of the students; it is also reflected in the age and maturity of the students. As a result, law school students bring their unique perspectives into the classroom, sharing their various life experiences after receiving various undergraduate, master's and even doctorate degrees, and after working in various professions prior to entering law school.

While this diversity enhances the law school environment by exposing both students and faculty to various ideologies and viewpoints, it can also present a number of challenges for the student and for the classroom.

From Undergraduate School to Law School

Many students choose to continue in their education and attend law school immediately after completing their undergraduate studies. While this may seem like the optimal plan for those interested in pursuing a law degree, students entering law school may struggle with the vast difference of this rigorous, academic environment. It will be even more profound for those attending the same institution for both undergraduate and law school as students might assume that the academic structure will remain the same.

One of the biggest changes that you will encounter in law school is the amount of time it requires. The days of partying all night and studying a couple of hours before an exam are over. Law school will impose on most of the free time you have outside of class. Expect to be challenged by a new way of thinking, reading and writing. Whatever you do, do not assume that because you did well in undergraduate school, law school will be easy. Your acceptance into law school means that you are a part of an elite group; your fellow classmates will have also graduated at the top of their class and received high scores on the LSAT. The hard work starts on day 1 and ends after you pass the bar exam. The fact that you are still in "school mode" will work in your favor since your classmates who have been out of school for awhile may require a longer adjustment period.

The Professional Student Meets Law School

Students entering law school after receiving other graduate degrees often find law school more challenging than those students entering law school directly after undergraduate school. As I mentioned before, law school is unlike any other graduate program. While you might assume that having a graduate degree will assist you in law school, it might actually make it more of a challenge as you struggle to adjust to the law school curriculum. The urge to compare law school to your prior graduate program will be strong. Avoid it and your transition will be much easier.

I remember a very lengthy conversation I once had with one of my first year students who came to law school after receiving his doctorate degree. Throughout the conversation, he talked about his struggle adjusting to law school and continuously compared his current educational experience with his previous ones. Having done well in his prior studies, he was convinced that he was not the problem. Instead, he opined that law school and its process of training students was the problem. After listening to his numerous suggestions on how law school should be changed to better assist its students in learning the material (banning the Socratic Method was first on his list), my recommendation to him was simple: accept that law school is different (it just is), stop focusing on how law school should change (because it will not) and start focusing on what will help him learn the material he would be required to apply on his exams.

If you are entering law school after completing another graduate program, know this: law school is different. Accept this, and move on. Focus on the challenges ahead of you, not the accomplishments behind you. It will make the transition into law school easier and the road in law school much smoother for you.

From One Profession to Another

Many students are coming to law school after several years in, and some even after retiring from a different career. Some of these students have held high-profile positions in their previous careers and are older than most people in their class, including the professor. Like students who have attended other graduate schools, starting a new career in law may prove to be arduous. The most common difficulty is adjusting to the different environment. It is not uncommon for those coming from previous academic and professional endeavors to rebel against and find fault with the uniqueness of law school. This is often evidenced through challenges of the law school learning process and those responsible for enforcing it. Some of these students spend valuable class time disputing the professor and case law and then later monopolize the professor's office time proving how much smarter they are than the law.

My advice to these students is to respect your fellow classmates, your professors and the classroom. As the precedent case law cannot be changed to conform to what you believe to be the right decision, learn from the lessons they impart and again, move on. Arguing with the professor does not further any goal in law school, it just distracts others trying to learn. If you have questions, ask them, but be respectful of the professor and your fellow classmates in the process. If you still have questions or need further clarification, talk to your professor during office hours or send an email after class.

Part-Time/Evening Students

If you are a part-time or evening student, who will be working full-time while in law school, let me first applaud you for taking on such an arduous endeavor. I am always amazed by my students who work during the day and attend classes until almost ten o'clock at night (and some even have to drive hours to and from school as well). Most of these students also have families and balance those responsibilities along with work and law school. Although some assume that law school is easier for part-time students, law school is law school and the task ahead is strenuous. Also, most part-time and evening programs are year-round to accommodate the reduced course load. Accordingly, in addition to the complications of law school, it will feel like it will never end.

Part-time and evening law students must plan carefully to maximize their success in law school. Although I will discuss time-management in greater detail later, one quick tip is to utilize the weekends to do the majority of your class work. Even though you likely excel at multi-tasking, I want to caution you against thinking that sleeping and eating are luxuries. Proportion your time so that you obtain a sufficient amount of rest and nutrients to maintain your hectic schedule.

Old Family, Meet New Family

It is not uncommon for students to have families, or even start a family, while in law school. Many students are single parents; some are married, but are sole caretakers for their children, and others are just starting on their parenting journey as new or expectant parents. On the other end of the spectrum, some students are taking care of their parents or grandparents. This can lead to challenges as students try to balance studying and adjusting to the new and rigorous law school environment, while maintaining the responsibilities of family life. Law school is extremely demanding. Before making the commitment to begin law school, make sure that you have considered and allotted for the tremendous amount of time that must be devoted to your studies and discussed the potential impact with your family.

Factor in the ages of your children and child care needed as you prepare to enter law school. If you have young children, do you have babysitting or childcare arranged at night to allow you to study and prepare for the next day's classes? Law school requires much more time studying and preparing for classes beyond the actual time that you spend in the classroom. This may be hard for a young child to comprehend. Having childcare assistance or a routine created which helps you to study after hours without interruption will be very beneficial.

If you have children in school, make sure you have childcare arranged in the event that your children are out of school for a teacher workday, inclement weather (just because your children's classes are cancelled does not mean that yours will be as well), illness or any other adverse condition. Bringing your children to law school should not be considered as a back-up in the event that your children are unable to attend school. Law school is not a playground or daycare. Even if you have the best behaved children who will sit quietly and not attempt to disturb you or your fellow classmates while they are there, it is not appropriate. In the event that an emergency mandates that you have no other alternative and have to bring your child to class with you, ask your professor well in advance of class (not while he or she is walking *into* the class) if it is permissible.

A fellow professor shared with me his horror in discovering a young, school-aged child in his class while he lectured on the differences in the various levels of rape and sexual assault. His lecture, which he described as extremely detailed and contained sexually-explicit language, was appropriate for adults, but certainly not appropriate for a young child. Although he was gracious about the unexpected guest and even apologized to the parent after the class, your professor might not be as accepting as this professor was. The professor should not have to alter the substance of a lecture because a student brought a child to class.

The most common problem that I hear among students with families who are having problems in school is the lack of support that they receive from their spouse or significant other. While initially supportive while you are applying to law school, some spouses and significant others cannot understand how difficult law school is or how much time it requires unless they have been to law school themselves. In the event that they have another graduate degree, they will even be less understanding of the time that you have to study as they may think that law school is similar to the program which they completed. As much as possible, prepare everyone who will be affected by your decision to attend law school for what the next three years will consist of. Make sure that you have their full support and enlist their help in the journey. The one thing that you cannot afford to do is sacrifice your sleep, sanity and self to maintain the status quo of how things were before you went to law school. This will only result in an emotional or mental breakdown later on (and it always seems to happen right before you take your exams).

Please do not misunderstand. It is possible to have a family and be successful in law school. You just have to plan and strive harder to make everything work. Although I waited to have children until right after law school, I had several classmates who had young children while in law school. It amazed me to see them manage it all, some even doing so without any support system at home to help them. They are proof that it can be done. These students all graduated and are now successful attorneys.

Students, whether traditional or non-traditional, will undoubtedly experience difficulties while in law school. The professors, while not unsympathetic to the challenges that some students face, are there to do their job. When problems arise, talk to your advisor, dean of student services or other law school support personnel to assist you in reaching a solution. Someone has probably encountered your problem before and these individual will be in a position to offer you additional assistance and support.

"A mind that is stretched by a new experience can never go back to its old dimensions."

-Oliver Wendell Holmes, Jr.

Chapter 2

The Beginning

Law school is a different world; it is unique and will be different from your prior educational experiences. Everything from the textbooks (called casebooks) to the way information is presented in class (Socratic Method) is different. Even the class years have different names. Everyone is familiar with "freshman," and "sophomore," but in law school years, students are labeled as "1L," "2L," and "3L."[1]

If you are anything like me, your prior knowledge of law school is limited to what you have heard from exaggerated and fictionalized versions from novels, movies and television shows. But, there is nothing like experiencing it in real life. Even speaking to former law students does not provide an accurate account of the "1L experience" as they are so far removed from their first year that their memories are blurred by their more recent, fonder experiences. As the saying goes, "time heals all wounds." How else would you explain why women, after experiencing the excruciating pain of childbirth (even with the "good" drugs), would choose to experience it again (and sometimes again, and again, and again)?

Orientation

You may remember orientation in your undergraduate school: a little bit of work; a lot of play and your first taste of true freedom. Orientation in law school, however, is not a fun-filled, "meet and greet" week to relax. Law school orientation translates into attending classes disguised as "introductions to the legal process," learning how to read and brief cases, getting an introduction to legal writing, and even doing homework. You will also hear from various offices such as the registrar, financial aid, career services, academic support and

---

[1] For students attending a law school evening program, years will be labeled 1LE, 2LE, 3LE and 4LE.

student services. You may also be introduced to the various student organizations and opportunities for involvement in the school and the surrounding community.

Ignore the urge to hold on to the last days of your summer by wearing shorts and t-shirts during orientation. Make sure that you have professional attire readily available because you will likely take pictures for the student directory. The directory is distributed to your fellow classmates, professors and potential employers. You do not want to have a picture represent you as a future attorney with you wearing a t-shirt and a borrowed blazer from the person in line in front of you. (If you do take pictures, make sure to smile. Remember that your future employers may be basing their hiring on your resume and photo. You do not want their first –and maybe only—impression to be based on a frown or smirk.) Also, make sure that you pay close attention to the tours of the building conducted during orientation because you will likely be too intimidated to ask where (and what) is the moot courtroom once the semester begins. Whether your law school has a brief two-day orientation program or a week of activities, treat orientation as a snapshot of your first semester and realize that you need to be ready to work from the very beginning.

Casebooks

You should already have a book list by now and your professors have likely already posted syllabi and reading assignments for the first week of class. This is where the similarities between undergraduate school and law school end. Textbooks in law school are called casebooks, and instead of having chapters filled with definitions, rules, and legal history, they are filled with written decisions of judges from actual court cases. New law students often find the reading to be difficult in part because some of the cases are at least one hundred years-old and are filled with "legalese." "Legalese" is "the jargon characteristically used by lawyers, esp.[ecially] in legal documents."[2] The use of "legalese" is what makes law school feel so foreign in the beginning. You may sit down to start reading your first case and wonder, "Did I buy the book in a different language?" For example, read the excerpt below from a case that is often assigned in the first semester of Property Law:

---

[2] Black's Law Dictionary 913 (8th ed. 2004).

I admit with *Fleta*, that pursuit alone does not give a right of property in animals *ferae naturae*, and I admit also that occupancy is to give a title to them. But then, what kind of occupancy? And here I shall contend it is not such as is derived from manucaption alone. In *Puffendorf's Law of Nature and of Nations*, b.4 c. 4 s. 5 n. 6 by *Barbeyrac*, notice is taken of this principle of taking possession. It is there combated, nay, disproved; and in b.4 c.6 s. 2 n.2 *Ibid.* s. 7 n. 2 demonstrated that manucaption is only one of many means to declare the intention of exclusively appropriating that, which was before in a state of nature. Any continued act which does this, is equivalent to occupancy. Pursuit, therefore, by a person who starts a wild animal, given as exclusive right whilst it is followed. It is all the possession the nature of the subject admits; it declares the intention of acquiring dominion, and is as much to be respected as manucaption itself. The contrary idea, requiring actual taking, proceeds, as Mr. *Barbeyrac* observes, in *Puffendorf,* b. 4 c. 6 s. 10 on a "false notion of possession."[3]

If you understood that this case was about fox hunting and who can claim ownership to wild animals, then give yourself an "A" for the day. If you did not understand the excerpt, you are likely in the majority. Do not get frustrated and think that you made the wrong decision by coming to law school. Just like it takes time to learn a foreign language, it takes time to learn and understand "legalese." There is a movement by some in the legal community towards using "plain English"[4] in legal writing, but as a first year law student you need to be aware that this movement is fairly recent and there are hundreds of court opinions that are written in the more formal "legalese."

Case Method/Socratic Method

When you are called on in class and you are put in the "hot seat," know that you can thank Christopher Columbus Langdell for your

---

[3] Pierson v. Post, 3 Cai. R. 175, 2 Am.Dec. 264 (1805).

[4] LAUREL CURRIE OATES ET AL., THE LEGAL WRITING HANDBOOK: ANALYSIS, RESEARCH, AND WRITING, 668 (3rd ed. 2002).

discomfort. Professor Langdell was Dean of Harvard Law School in the late 1800's and while he was not the first to use the Case Method,[5] he was pivotal in leading law school professors around the country to employ this style of teaching. Dean Langdell also replaced the Lecture Method[6] with the Socratic Method,[7] named after the Greek philosopher, Socrates. The combined Case Method/Socratic Method is most commonly used today in law schools across the country. Instead of passively sitting in your seat taking notes on the professor's lecture topic and then later regurgitating your notes on the final exam, you will engage in an active dialogue between you, your classmates, and the professor. Not only will you be asked to discuss the basic details about the cases assigned, you will also be required to answer new questions, hypotheticals, (fictional fact scenarios, designed to test your knowledge of the rules and then the application of the rule), posed by the professor by applying the same reasoning from the cases. Do not expect your professor to tell you if your reasoning was right or wrong; most likely he or she will just continue to ask you more questions. I cannot remember the number of times I was told that the Socratic Method was important because it teaches you to "think like a lawyer." At that point, I was simply "thinking like a first-year law student" and wanted to have my professor tell me what the right answer was (or at least let me know if I was on the right track). Sometimes, despite reading the cases prior to class, attending class, and listening to the discussion, you may still leave the room with no clue about what is going on. Do not get frustrated. This process is designed to strengthen your critical thinking skills and it is not a personal attack on you by your professor. The fear of the "hot seat" will probably stay with you throughout the first year of law school; but know that you are making the first step in your transition as a lawyer and pretty soon you will speak, write and think like one.

---

[5] The Case Method (also termed as the Casebook Method, Case System and Langdell Method) as "an inductive system of teaching law in which students study specific cases to learn general legal principles." BLACK'S LAW DICTIONARY at 228.

[6] Also called the Hornbook Method, the Lecture Method is "a method of legal instruction characterized by a straightforward presentation of legal doctrine, occasionally interspersed with questions." Id. at 754.

[7] "A technique of philosophical discussion – and of law instruction –by which the questioner (a law professor) questions one or more followers (the law students), building on each answer with another question, esp. an analogy incorporating the answer." Id. at 1425.

"There is one kind of robber whom the law does not strike at, and who steals what is most precious to men: time."

-Napoleon Bonaparte

Chapter 3

Adjusting to Law School

"The law is a jealous mistress," I was warned when I shared with an acquaintance my intention to leave the teaching profession to attend law school. As a practicing attorney, I found that statement to be true. Being a lawyer requires a lot of time and attention. It is only fitting then that the matriculation through law school is as demanding –if not more –than the practice of law itself.

Time Management

Law school requires a considerable amount of time and work. As early as your first week, you will realize that law school is not just a *part* of your life, where you spend a couple hours in classes each day, five days a week; it *is* your life, consuming most of your time the entire day, seven days of week (and yes, even including breaks and holidays). I cannot remember a night in my first or second year when I did not have something to do for one of my classes; it felt like there was always more reading, briefing, studying or other preparation for classes than there were hours in the day to accomplish it all. Often times, I felt I had enough work for just one class to keep me occupied all night. The amount of time required for *all* of my classes combined seemed impossible.

To be successful in law school, you must be prepared. Time management is crucial to that preparation. Law school is like a full-time job. Knowing how to budget your time will be an asset to you in law school, and it will also assist you post-law school when you prepare for the ultimate test of your law school knowledge, the bar exam.

Making a Schedule

To effectively manage your time, the first thing you should do is make a schedule. This schedule should be as detailed as possible and should incorporate the following: attending classes, reading and preparing for the next day's classes, studying individually and meeting with your study group, in addition to those necessities such as eating, sleeping and winding down. While there are sample schedules readily available, use those solely as a template in creating your own personal schedule. Write your schedule down on paper and post it where you can see it and reference it often during the day. If you create your schedule electronically, make sure you print it out and post it someplace where you will constantly see it, or keep it in your daily planner. Having it in front of you will make it much easier for you to refer to it and abide by it, rather than having to turn on your computer each time you need to reference it. Your law school should provide you with an academic calendar which includes all holidays, breaks, study days, and exam days. Incorporate the academic schedule into your schedule, as well as the assignments on the syllabi provided by your professors. If you have a writing assignment or research assignment due, allot sufficient time in your schedule to work on the assignment, in addition to the regular study time that you have apportioned for your classes.

Many students ask how much time they should spend studying. This will vary depending on the subject, but generally, you should try to spend approximately three hours studying for every one hour of class. For example, if you are taking fifteen credit hours, you should devote at least forty-five hours each week to studying[8] (remember, law school has become your full time job). Studying time will include reading and briefing cases, reviewing your class notes and developing outlines. Spread this time out over the course of the week. Do not establish bad habits by "cramming" your study time for a particular class into one night. While the preferred method is to read and brief cases during the week and outline and study on the weekends, some students prefer to use the weekends to get as much of the weekly assignments done so that their time during the week can be spent studying substantive material. Your course syllabus should provide you with the cases or materials that will be covered during each class period so you can study and prepare well in advance of each class. Make your schedule according to what works best for you.

Decide on a time each night when all work will be completed (your shut down time). Although sleeping and eating may seem to be a luxury, they are necessary for your brain and the rest of your body to

---

[8] This figure is calculated by comparing the amount of time that a student should devote to law school to the average attorney work week of sixty hours.

function at the capacity that it needs for law school. Adding in exercise or some other healthy extra-curricular activity will allow you to reset and rejuvenate.

After you make the schedule, try to adhere to it as much as possible. After the first week of using your schedule, note how your time was actually spent. At the end of the week, compare your original schedule with your notes of how your time was *actually* spent to determine how and why the schedules varied. This may seem like a pointless exercise but the extra few minutes it takes you to chart out your time will be very beneficial, allowing you to see how and where you are spending your time (versus how you *should* be spending your time). You can then make adjustments if you are spending too much time on one activity and not enough on another. The more you adhere to your schedule, the greater the likelihood that you will have enough time to accomplish everything. Once you have finalized your schedule you can begin to establish a routine for balancing class time and free time.

Of course, you cannot predict the unexpected events that may require you to deviate from your schedule. Life does not stop just because you are in law school. If you have a minor event, getting back on track should be easy to do. However, many students will have to deal with major, life-altering events while in law school that may have a greater impact on their schedule. If this happens to you, use the resources available at your law school to help. As discussed in more detail in a later chapter, many law schools have dedicated personnel to assist students in dealing with issues that arise during law school that may have an effect on their studies. Do not wait until an event becomes a crisis to talk to your professors and/or law school administrators. By then, it may be too late for them to provide any assistance. If a situation arises which gets you off your schedule, while it may be more difficult to resume your normal schedule, but it is never impossible.

Working in Law School

One thing that you will notice that I did not suggest for you to incorporate into your schedule is outside work.[9] Until you have a grasp

---

[9] Of course this only applies to students who are enrolled in a full-time program. It is understood that the majority of part-time students will attend law school while working full-time.

of exactly what is required of you in law school, you should postpone any plans for part-time work. If possible, do not work at all in law school, especially during your first year. It is important to establish a good foundation your first year. In order to do that, you must be able to devote your full time and attention to law school. If you feel that you absolutely have to work, check with your law school first to make sure that it is allowed. The American Bar Association prohibits a student enrolled full time (in excess of twelve hours) in law school from working more than twenty hours per week in any week.[10] Some law schools may impose a greater restriction on working than what is permitted by the American Bar Association.

Support Systems

In order to be successful at managing your time and sticking to your schedule, you must have the support of family and friends. Before beginning law school, talk to your friends and family about how much it means to you to attend law school, and, most importantly, to do well. Law school is a tremendous commitment, but it is, thankfully, only a three-year commitment. Share with your significant other, family and friends how your time will be limited and how much effort law school will require. It also helps to have those who are close to you to become a part of your commitment. One of my students shared how her best friend made her home-cooked soup, froze it and shipped it overnight to her to ensure that she was eating and did not have to take time out of her schedule to cook (what a friend that was). Your family and friends should be your partners in this new endeavor. Ask them to assist you in being accountable and adhering to your schedule. They will then feel like they are a part of the process and can share in your accomplishments. Be firm in your commitment, and others will see how serious you are about being successful in law school. They, in turn, will be supportive and understanding of the time that you will need to dedicate to studying. Let those who are close to you know that when you are studying, you are not to be disturbed. Do not take phone calls, read or answer emails or text messages or engage in other non-law school related activities while studying. Learn how to say no to other people and other things that interfere with your school time and study time. This is not to say that you cannot incorporate time

---

[10] American Bar Association 2009-2010 Standards 304(f).

with your friends and family into your schedule. As a reward for all your studying, treat yourself to a date night or a night out on the town each week with friends.[11] This time-off will help you to maintain a healthy balance between law school and life outside of law school. One caveat, however; although you will undoubtedly have made lots of new friends in law school, try to have balance and use that time to catch-up with your friends outside of law school. This will prevent you from using your time-off to talk about school-related things (it's supposed to be time "off," remember).

---

[11] Be careful not to go overboard with your time off and party so hard that you have to use the rest of the weekend to recuperate instead of studying.

"In the middle of difficulty lies opportunity."

-Albert Einstein

Chapter 4

Preparing for Class

Law School Curriculum

Ask any law school graduate what the most difficult year in law school was and more often than not, the answer will be the first year. According to statistics provided by the American Bar Association, in the 2007-2008 Academic Year, out of the total number of students who left law school prior to obtaining a juris doctorate degree, 75.9% were first year students, compared to 20.3% of second year students, 3.4% of third year students and .04% of 4th year students.[12] This can be attributed in part to some students not having a clear understanding of what to expect in law school, but it is also largely due to the difficult course load for first year students. Your first year of law school will consist of a set curriculum for all first-year law students at your school. Most law schools provide the curriculum for first-year students on their websites. Although the curriculum for first-year students may vary slightly depending on the law school, most law schools have the following required courses for all first-year students:

Civil Procedure-"The body of law-usually rules enacted by the legislature or courts-governing the methods and practices used in civil litigation."[13]

Constitutional Law-"The body of law deriving from the U.S. Constitution and dealing primarily with governmental powers, civil rights, and civil liberties."[14]

Contracts- The law concerning the formulation of agreements "between two or more parties creating obligations that are enforceable or otherwise recognizable at law."[15]

---

[12] http://www.abanet.org/legaled/statistics/charts/stats%20-%2017.pdf

[13] BLACK'S LAW DICTIONARY at 263.

[14] Id. at 331.

[15] Id. at 341.

Criminal Law-"The body of law defining offenses against the community at large, regulating how suspects are investigated, charged, and tried, and establishing punishments for convicted offenders."[16]

Legal Analysis, Research and Writing- A course which introduces the intricacies of legal research and analysis and assists the students in honing their legal writing skills.

Property Law-The law concerning a person's "right to possess, use, and enjoy a determinate thing (either a tract of land or a chattel)."[17]

Torts- The law concerning "[a] civil wrong, other than breach of contract, for which a remedy may be obtained, usually in the form of damages; a breach of a duty that the law imposes on persons who stand in a particular relation to one another."[18]

Reading Cases

Each class will require a tremendous amount of reading, which will at first seem insurmountable. Because you have so much reading, it is important that you maximize the time you spend reading for each class. Read for comprehension, not just for the sake of reading. Many cases will contain unfamiliar words. Invest in a good legal dictionary and look up all words that you do not know. This will help you to understand the text as well as assist you with building your legal vocabulary. Read the information in the text, as well as any prefatory information, which is located within the footnotes and information at the end of each case or chapter.[19] Your reading may also refer to the holding from another case or a statute. Read the information that the book provides you about that case or statute (or if that information is not enough for you to gain a clear understanding of the material, you may need to pull up the case or statute). In the beginning you may have to re-read cases several times to understand the material. Be sure to take notes while you read and notate anything that you believe will be important in any class discussion. You may also want to read supplemental materials for further clarification and understanding.

---

[16] Id. at 403.

[17] Id. at 1252.

[18] Id. at 1526.

[19] Do not ignore the concurring and dissenting opinions that follow the majority opinion. They provide valuable information and insight about the cases and/or law.

Briefing Cases

Your orientation or first week of law school will probably included a lesson on case briefing. Briefing cases helps you to identify the important information within each case. Your class briefs are primarily a summary of the assigned reading and they should contain enough information to refresh your memory on what you have read. Although there are several different ways to brief a case, the essential elements of briefing are: providing the facts of the case, (which includes identifying the parties), identifying the issue, stating the rule(s) of law, analyzing/applying the rule with the facts of the case and then summarizing the case through a statement of the court's holding and other pertinent information regarding the final disposition of the case.

When briefing, use the format provided to you by your instructors, or recommended by the law school. Professors in the beginning of the first year will probably call on students to brief cases for class. Having this information in front of you will maximize your ability to provide your professor with the exact information requested, instead of wasting your time, your classmates' time and most importantly, the professor's time, trying to locate the information within the text.

Although briefing is time consuming, it enables you to present the information in an organized and concise manner so that the material is easier to understand and apply. The more you brief, the easier and quicker the process will become. It may be tempting to circumvent briefing by simply trying to highlight the important text in the book while reading or by writing notes in the margin of the cases. [20] Avoid this temptation, as it will not assist you in developing the necessary skills that you will need later in law school and in the practice of law: the ability to analyze cases and extract the essential information from the text for a particular purpose.

Now, a word about using commercial briefs (often referred to as "canned" briefs) for classes. There is an abundance of reference material available on-line and in bookstores that correspond with your cases and reading material. These materials are supplementary and should be used exactly for that purpose, to *supplement* your learning.

---

[20] This method is called "book briefing" and it is not the most efficient way to prepare for class discussions.

Your professors are very much aware of the existence of these materials as they receive complimentary copies of texts and supplementary material from publishers. As they know what is contained in these materials, they recognize the key words and phrases used in the canned briefs. They will know whether you are reciting information that is your own because you have done the work, or your own because you have purchased it.

There will undoubtedly be well-meaning 2Ls and 3Ls who will want to assist you by providing you with their briefs from their previous classes. When I was in law school, we were all assigned mentors during our first year to assist us with the transition into law school. Students would rate their mentors based on the amount of materials they would pass along to them. In study groups, we would have mounds of material to compare, share and discuss with each other and would copy all the information of our study partners and leave with a bigger stack of papers than we came in with.

In the age of modern technology, the material can be found with the click of a mouse. You can conveniently access briefs written by students who have not only taken the class, but who also had the same professor that you have (how much better can it get, right?). I have heard stories of rising 2Ls passing around a USB drive with all the briefs for the required first year courses on them for 1Ls to upload onto their computer. In one law school, 2Ls held their own orientation for 1Ls and handed out CDs with all briefs, outlines and old exams for all 1L courses.[21] Again, this information should be used to supplement your own materials. Never use these materials to replace your reading, briefing or other preparation for class. Additionally, it takes a lot of time to read supplementary materials. This time is better spent studying the assigned materials. Those that do well in law school do so because they worked hard and do not take shortcuts. Your degree of

---

[21] One of my first-year students came into my office in the middle of the first semester asking whether it was really a good investment of her time to brief cases and to make her own outlines for class. One of her friends, who was in her second year, called it "reinventing the wheel," and felt that the time should be spent studying the pre-prepared material instead. Although I gave her my standard advice that taking the time to prepare your own materials will never be a waste of time, she chose to use brief and outlines already prepared instead of making her own. The next semester, I ran into her and asked how she did. Although she thought it went well, she felt she could have done much better had she done her own briefing and outlining.

success in law school will correspond directly with the amount of th. and effort you put into it. Although it may seem too early to think about it, most large firms only recruit students for internships (which lead to formal job offers) who have a certain GPA. Doing well your first year will better position you for greater opportunities beyond your first year.

"Today's preparation determines tomorrow's achievement."

-Unknown

Chapter 5

What to Do While in Class

Taking Notes

Effective note-taking during class is a critical skill for law school success. So far, a lot of what you have read in this book is new information, unique to the law school experience. Since this chapter is about note-taking, a skill that you have already mastered since you have come this far, you are probably thinking you can skip it. Please avoid the temptation, because just like everything else, you need a different approach on how to take and use your class notes in law school. If you take notes properly then it will make your exam preparation easier. Specifically, your class notes should serve as your roadmap and should guide you through the complex material.

Taking good notes in class serves several functions. The first and probably the most important function is making you an active listener instead of a passive one. Active listening requires you to focus on to whom and what you are listening. As an active listener, you should be able to repeat back, in your own words, what the speaker said to reflect your understanding. Reading and briefing cases prior to class also assists you when it is time to listen and take notes as the material discussed in class will not be new information, but rather a review of concepts and information you have obtained from your independent or group study. If you are not taking notes and are simply sitting in class trying to "take it all in," you become a passive listener instead of an active one (of course checking your email, surfing the web, playing games on your computer and instant messaging your friends definitely falls in the passive or non-listener category). Passive listeners, even those who are not distracted by other activities, tend to get less out of the class than those who are actively taking part in the class discussion.

A second function of note-taking is that having good notes will help you understand points in the cases that were not clear to you before class. You will often find that your brief does not contain the key points that your professor considers important. Sometimes you may even wonder if you have briefed the right case because you are so far off-base and confused about what you read. Do not despair, just make sure that you edit your brief during class and add and delete information as needed.[22] Your "final" brief should contain the key facts, the issue(s), rules, and other important information from each case. A third function of note-taking is that it helps to reinforce the information in your mind, so that you are more likely to remember it during the exam.

When you are taking notes, it is important to think about what you are writing down, because not every word spoken in class is worthy of space on your paper. You want to make sure you write down what your professor is saying, particularly if there is no Socratic Method and the professor begins to lecture. This is the time that your professor provides you with key definitions and rules. But, since this is not a regular occurrence in most classes, you need to listen and take note of the hypotheticals. You also want to take note of any recurring phrases, statements or legal "terms of art."[23] Finally, you want to take note of any discussion of policy or rationale behind the applicable rules.

If you find yourself taking note of your classmates' comments, make sure that you distinguish their comments from the professor's. Sometimes your classmates will say something very insightful and important, but most of the time they are in the same boat you are in and they are just as confused as you are. Set up your own "filter" and pick a way to identify what came from your professor and what came from the person who likes to talk in every class. I suggest that you use a different colored pen, write "PROF" in front of any comments made by your professor or highlight the professor's comments. If may take you awhile before you feel confident with your ability to gauge what is important to write down during class. The process is a little like

---

[22] I used the split-page method to brief cases in law school. I would write my brief on the right half of the page and save the left side to take notes, correct errors in my brief, and jot down hypotheticals. Some days I would have to mark through my entire brief and rewrite it on the left side because I did not hit the correct issues, rules, etc.

[23] A term of art is "[a] word or phrase having a specific, precise meaning in a given specialty, apart from its general meaning in ordinary context. BLACK'S LAW DICTIONARY at 1511.

Goldilocks and the Three Bears; you cannot write too much or too little but you have to fine tune what you do until it is just right. Also, do not panic if you get lost during class. Leave a signal like a question mark and some space in your notes. Come back later to fill in the holes. Regardless of what you write or how you distinguish your professor's comments from your own and your classmates', the goal is for your class notes to tell you what your professor considers important, and therefore, what is likely to tested on the exam.

Typing vs. Handwriting

Nowadays, when you look in a law school classroom, you see the majority of the students typing away on their laptops during class. A computer is an essential tool for law school but there is serious debate on whether the use of computers in class helps the student focus. Some typists end up acting as court stenographers, they type every word spoken in class and inevitably are unable to follow the class discussion because they are in the typing zone. One of the biggest complaints students raise about writing is that they cannot write fast enough, but that is a plus in class because it allows you to be more selective about what you write down. You tend to listen more closely, which helps you with your understanding. Also, you can increase your speed if you create your own shorthand or use common abbreviations for legal terms.

What a waste of your time to take all of those notes and then fail to review them. One of the best and easiest ways to maximize your retention of the information from class is to read your notes immediately after class (or at least within the next 24 to 48 hours) and fill in any blanks. By doing this, you want to transfer the information from your "short-term" memory to your "long-term" memory before your forget it. Additionally, if you do not review your notes shortly after taking them, odds are you will not remember what all those question marks represent and you will not be able to fill in those blanks when it's time to prepare for your finals. Finally, I suggest that you try to summarize the day's class in a sentence or two. This technique allows you to self-assess your grasp of the material you covered in class and determine if you understand it or if you need to clarify a point with a classmate or your professor.[24]

---

[24] Do not worry if you do not understand the material after the end of each class, sometimes it takes several class sessions to grasp the concepts.

"If you want something, don't wish for it, work for it."

-Stephen Hines

Chapter 6

Preparing for Exams

Now that you have this information, what do you do with it all? How do you best maximize your time to make the most of all the information that you have? There are several methods that you can implement to organize and compile all your information. If used, these will be very helpful as you prepare for your final exams.

Outlines

One of the most widely used study materials is a course outline that compiles all the information that you have gathered from different sources. Outlining will help you to understand, process, and study all the material that you have accumulated. When you do begin to study for the final exam, it will be invaluable to have all your information in one location, rather than going back and forth between your books, notes and various materials to study. Your outline should incorporate information from your readings, cases, class lectures and tutorials. Make time in your schedule to outline each week, as it is easier to outline as you go, rather than all at once at the end of the semester.

Your outline does not have to be formal. You do not have to use complete sentences or follow the outline "format" with Roman Numerals followed by capital letters, then numbers, then small caps, etc. It is imperative, however, that your outline is organized. Having a bunch of material on a piece of paper without any structure will be more harmful to you than if you chose not to outline at all. Use bullets and indentations to help you organize your material. Use your syllabus as a guide in outlining. Organize information according to the subject or rules from your cases and notes. Be sure to include any exceptions to the rule in your outline. Highlight or underline important information that your professor emphasizes to you in class (this will often be the information that he/she uses to come up with questions for your final exam).

As I mentioned in Chapter 4, there will be an abundance of commercial products and handed-down materials—including outlines—that will be available to you from stores and other students. Again, use these materials to *supplement* your own outlining. No amount of commercial or second-hand material can prepare you for your final exams as well as your own outlining. Remember, law school, like everything else in life, is like a bank. You get out of it, what you get into it (and sometimes with interest); the more you put into it, the more you will get out of it. Those that put in the time and effort to do their own outlining will reap the benefits of it. The individuals that authored the supplementary outlines certainly have put in the time and effort and most likely have a law degree (and a good job making these commercial outlines). Please do not misunderstand. I am not trying to put those who make, market and mass produce these outlines out of business. They can be extremely helpful as you gather as much material as you can to fill in any gaps in your understanding of a particular concept so you can prepare your *own* study guides. Just do not use them to replace your own work as there is no substitute for the knowledge you will gain from making your own outlines.

Flashcards

Flashcards are another method to help you learn material. Use flashcards for legal terms, concepts and theories from your reading and class notes. Take the key elements from your outline and put the material on flashcards. Like outlining, make the flashcards as you go along, rather than all at once. Making flashcards may seem elementary but it is a great way to study and test your knowledge of key information. This is also a way you can involve your significant others in your studying by having them go through the flashcards with you. (It probably will help them see the mass amount of information that you have to learn; they will be more understanding when you have to sacrifice time with them for studying.) The flashcards will be helpful not only as you study for the final exam, but when you gather all your law school materials when you prepare for the bar exam. Commercial flashcards are also available for all core law classes. Be advised, however, that these are general in nature and may not contain key concepts and information discussed in the course casebook or given to you by your professor in class.

Match Your Study Method to Your Learning Style

There are other methods to assist you in studying and processing all of the material you are required to learn. Everyone has a different learning style. Find out what helps you the most to remember and memorize information. Use what works best for you. If you are a visual learner, make visual aids to illustrate legal concepts and organize key information. Make flowcharts, timelines or other diagrams that explain and categorize information. Provide a history of case law or legislation. If you are an auditory learner, try putting your outlines and other information in an audio format to use as a study aid. If you have a long commute to your law school, you can play a CD while you drive to maximize the use of your time in the car (and now you can even find legal resources to download on your MP3 player to have access to your law school material 24/7). If you are a kinesthetic and/or tactile learner, you learn best by incorporating movement with your studying. Even something as simple as pacing the room while you review your study materials or tapping your foot while you sit and read can increase your focus and retention of the information. If you haven't already done so, take the time find out what your learning style is because it will enable you to maximize your time with a study method that best suits your individual needs. [25]

Study Groups

Study groups are another valuable tool to further enhance your law school learning. Study groups are small groups of people in your class who meet routinely to compare notes, review material and study for each class. In these groups students review outlines, discuss and clarify information from classes. They quiz each other on legal concepts, practice multiple choice questions and essays and review supplementary material together.

This core group of people will be the equivalent of your family in law school. Although you will interact and sometimes study with other friends and classmates, your study group will be your main source of support and peer learning throughout law school. My study group was formed on the first day of orientation before I even really knew the people that would be my study partners for the next three years.

---

[25] To determine your learning style see http://www.vark-learn.com/english/page.asp?p=questionnaire

I remember being asked by a fellow student I sat next to during orientation to be in his study group after an upperclassman law student encouraged us to get in a study group. From there, we asked two others that we had casual conversations with during orientation (and who looked just as scared and clueless as we did) to join us. That is how our study group was formed. Although it worked well for us, we were extremely lucky considering the lack of planning and thought that goes into choosing study group members. There were other students in law school that did not fare as well in their selections. Some students went through several different groups of people before they found the right fit for them. There were even students who were unhappy in their study group and had no group to join and ended up without a core group of students to work with throughout this arduous endeavor.

Choose your study group carefully. Do not select people based on friendship, but rather on their learning styles, work ethic and what they can contribute to the group. One of my students told me that she was actually interviewed by her study group prior to being allowed to become a member. After she was accepted, she was given a "trial membership period" so that the other group members could make sure that she was pulling her weight prior to being given full membership status. While that may seem extreme, it made this student feel confident that this was the right group. These students took their work seriously and were determined to be in the top of their class.

If your law school has different sections, it may be a good idea to have people from different sections in your study group, as you can benefit from the different perspectives offered from the professors in that section. If you study best at night, choose classmates that are night owls like you to be in your study group. Find others who have the same goals and will provide encouragement, support and tough love, if necessary, so that you can help each other to accomplish those goals.

Your study group should be small in number. My study group had four members and it seemed to be a perfect number. Groups with more than five members will be too difficult to coordinate and may be counterproductive when trying to work through the material. Plan to meet with your study group at least once a week for several hours.[26]

---

[26] A number of my students in the evening program use modern technology to meet "virtually" with their study group members using message boards, web-based video conferencing and other social networks.

Meet at the same time and on the same day(s) each week. Treat these meetings like class and only miss your study group if there is absolutely no way to prevent it. Respect your study group partners by being on time and prepared to contribute in the review and discussion. Although some law students think that they will fare better in law school by studying alone, they should be aware that a study group is not just about studying: it is a forum to share and review information from class. If used correctly, being involved in a study group can greatly enhance learning in law school. However, avoid the pitfall of turning your study group into a social hour. Schedule times outside of your designated study group time (or even the first or last fifteen minutes of each session) for you to socialize and "catch up" with each other. This will allow you to keep a "work only" policy while studying with your group. Adhering to this policy will ensure that everyone receives the most benefits out of your study group time.

Develop activities that allow all members to learn from each other and participate. One suggested activity for study groups is to do practice drills where you call out a topic and everyone will type or write out as many of the rules and exceptions they can recall in two minutes. At the end of two minutes, each person will share their responses. This activity allows each person to assess knowledge of the material, as well as learn from the other group members.

I do want to caution you, however, not to *overuse* your study group. The majority of your time studying should NOT be group studying. Your exam is not a "study group exam." *You* will be responsible for *your* knowledge and understanding of the material. Thus, spending thirty to forty hours a week in your study group, creating a group outline or practicing multiple choice questions as a group may result in you getting poor results on your exams.

Incorporating the above methods into your routine in your first year of law school will prove to be very beneficial as you as you work towards success in law school. As law school is different than undergraduate and other graduate programs, you will have to try different methods of studying to determine what works best for you in learning the information. Different courses may also require different forms of studying to learn the material. Whatever you do, do not give up. If one method does not work for you, keep searching until you find one, or a combination of different methods that will assist you.

"We are what we repeatedly do. Excellence, then is not an act, but a habit."

- Aristotle

Chapter 7

Taking Exams

Law School Exams

Just when you thought law school could not be hard enough, you find out that one exam will probably determine your grade for the entire course. If you are lucky, you attend a law school that offers midterms (even though you will not think you are so lucky when midterms roll around), but the majority of you will have one chance to prove how much you know. Since your exams are so important, you want to make sure you have a game plan before you sit down to take your first exam. Procrastination and cramming are your worst enemies in law school. If those methods worked for you before, do not fool yourself into thinking that they will work again. Exam preparation starts from the first day of class, by reading, briefing, going to class, taking good notes, and synthesizing the material with outlines, flash cards or flow charts. If you take these steps all semester, then your task to prepare for exams will be much more manageable.

One of the keys to exam preparation is to know what to expect on the exams. You need to find out the format of your exam – whether it will consist of objective (multiple-choice) questions, short answer questions, essays, or any number of combinations of these three. Additionally, your law school exams may be closed or open book. Some law schools administer in-class exams during the first year and take-home exams in subsequent years.

Also, you need to recognize that law school exams are different, in that these exams focus on a different set of skills than other academic exams. You are probably used to being tested on your ability to memorize information from your books or class lectures. In law school, there is a certain level of memorization of the "black-letter law" [27] (even though there are some who do not like to acknowledge

---

[27] Black-letter law is defined as "one or more legal principles that are old, fundamental, and well settled." BLACK'S LAW DICTIONARY at 180.

this), but the emphasis is on your analytical or critical thinking skills. Your law school exams will not test you on the facts and holdings of the cases in your books, nor will you have a section on the test where all you have to do is define and recite key rules discussed in class. The reality of your exams is that you will be tested on scenarios that have a foundation in what you read and hear in class. Again, the whole point of law school is to teach you to think like a lawyer. As a lawyer, you need to have the ability to listen to your client and discern what her legal issue is and what rules apply. The average client will not walk into your office and tell you precisely what her legal issue is, what she wants to sue for, what arguments to make and the arguments that the opposing side could make. Also, this future client of yours will rarely give you just the right amount of facts. In reality, you will either have to piece together the story from the limited facts she gives you, or determine the significant facts from all the extraneous information she shares with you.

Essay Exams

Writing a good law school essay answer requires strategy. In my experience, I have found that students who fail to learn and use good essay writing skills tend to receive disappointing grades. Good essay exam writing skills require that you: (1) read the question carefully; (2) properly allocate your time; (3) spot the issue(s); (4) properly analyze the issue(s); and (5) communicate your answer in a clear, organized manner. (Of course, these skills mean nothing if you do not know the substantive law – so pay attention to Chapter 6 and the suggestions on learning the rules.)

When you are taking essay exams, careful reading is one of the most important skills. It does not matter if you know the law, if you fail to read carefully. Most law school essays are filled with facts, (some are important and some are red herrings), but if you read too fast or only read the question once, you are setting yourself up for failure. Also, when you are reading the exam, make sure that you do not skip the instructions. Some students assume they will save time and skip the instructions, but your professor put them there for a reason. You do not want to be the one student who failed to write on every other page, skipped a line or missed the instruction to pick only two of the three essays to answer (all of the above REALLY HAVE HAPPENED to my students). One tip to help you with reading carefully is to start with the "call of the question" first (this is usually the last line or two at the end of the facts-what the question is asking you to do). Reading the call of the question helps you to focus on what you will need to analyze. Make sure you read the question more than once because even the most careful reader will not catch everything on the first read. While you are reading the fact pattern, be sure to mark it, paying special attention to dates, parties, locations, time, weather, ages, quantities, etc. Also look for key words or phrases that will trigger discussion of a particular legal issue.

After you have read the essay several times, you should map out your answer before you start writing. This allows you to take time to process the question before you write and increase your chances of correctly identifying and analyzing the issues. You should *quickly* jot down a skeleton outline or chart in sequential order of major issues first. In your brief outline you want to include the issue(s), the general rules that need to be discussed, note any exceptions, distinctions or limitations to the general rule and any defenses. Also, briefly make note of the key facts that apply to the rules that you have identified. Students frequently challenge this method and believe that it will take too much time, but it should only take about fifteen to twenty-five percent of your allotted time. When you take the time in the beginning to read carefully and outline, you will have a better organized answer. You can also manage your time during the exams by making sure you are aware of the content of the exam and that you do not spend a disproportionate amount of time on one question. Sometimes your professor will indicate the suggested time to allot to each question. This time allocation, unless otherwise denoted by your professor, provides the grading weight of a question.

After you have carefully read the question several times, and taken the time to outline your answer, you will write an organized essay answer. One of the challenges of law school exams for many students is not *what* to write but *how* to write it. Some of your professors might be specific and tell you that your answer should be written in a certain way, such as in an IRAC (issue, rule, analysis/application and conclusion) or a CRAC (conclusion, rule, analysis/application, conclusion). Some professors might have their own format that they want you to use; or you might have the professors who do not have a preference. Regardless of what method you use, the key to good essay writing is to organize your answer. IRAC or CRAC are just two of many ways to organize a law school essay answer but since they are the most common, I will go over them in detail.

IRAC/CRAC

Law school essays do not require an introductory paragraph, nor do they require a statement of the facts before you answer the call of the question. If you use the IRAC or CRAC format, then this will help you to dive right in. The IRAC starts with a brief statement of the issue or legal question that you have to answer. An example of this would be "The issue is whether Joe is liable for battery when he snatched the cane from Aunt Bea's hand and she immediately fell to the ground." The CRAC starts with a sentence which is a brief answer to the question posed at the end of the essay such as "Joe is liable for battery when he snatched the cane from Aunt Bea's hand and she immediately fell to the ground."[28]

The remaining sections of the IRAC and CRAC (rules, analysis/application and conclusion) are the same. The rule section is a statement of the applicable principles of law. You should state the rules with all the elements that you will need to resolve the issue(s) you are discussing. Also, when necessary, start with the general rules, then state the exceptions to the rules. One thing you want to avoid doing in your rule section is including every rule you can think of, regardless of whether it answers the legal question posed by your professors. Your rule section should just be a legal summary of the rules you will apply in the analysis section. Using the above example, your rule section would include the rule/elements of a battery under tort law.

The analysis/application is the "meat" of any law school essay exam. This section will likely be worth the most points on your professor's grade sheet. You will discuss and apply the key facts from the essay prompt to each element of the rule. The disputed elements should be the main focus of your answer, but depending on your professor, you might also need to explain why a particular rule does not apply. Most of your essay exams require you to remain objective and you cannot advocate for only one side. However, this does not mean you should not consider and present counter-arguments, when appropriate. Remember, in law there is never just one answer, so be prepared to consider both sides. You should look at the facts in

---

[28] Note: these are simplified forms of issue and conclusion statements. Your school may require a specific formula or format, (i.e. "Under...does...when..." or "The issue is whether...").

relation to the rule and ask whether the requirements of the rule have been satisfied or not. In the battery example, you would need to discuss each element of a battery and the applicable facts which tend to satisfy each element, as well as discuss under this scenario, what the element at issue is (here, whether the contact with the cane was sufficient to satisfy the element of bodily contact).

The last part of your essay answer is the conclusion section. This section should be brief and you do not want to address any rules or facts here. You need to directly answer the question raised in the issue section in your IRAC or restate your conclusion from the beginning of your CRAC (make sure that your conclusions in the CRAC match each other.

Objective/Multiple-Choice Questions

Objective questions, i.e. multiple-choice questions, also require strategy. But do not despair; the approach you should take is similar to essay questions. Like an essay, with a multiple-choice question you need to "spot" the issue and identify the applicable rule, but unlike the essay, there will only be one "right" answer. The first step for answering a multiple-choice question is the same as with the essay, you want to read the call of the question first. Next, you should go back to the beginning of the question and read the fact pattern. Law school multiple-choice questions tend to be long and detailed. Again, for the same reason as with the essay, this approach will help you narrow down and focus on the issue that needs to be addressed. Next, you should try to determine what the answer is before you read the answer choices. (I always recommend to my students to cover up the answer choices with their hands or paper.) Ask yourself what you think the applicable rule is and then decide what you think is the answer. The point of this strategy is that your professors will often include "tempting" choices that will sway you. (Remember, they are trained lawyers who have years of experience in making convincing arguments, so figure it out before you read the answers.) The final step in answering a multiple-choice question is to read the answer options and eliminate the incorrect responses. Hopefully, you will see an answer choice which is similar to what you have already determined the answer to be. If not, sometimes you have to go to the old, reliable process of elimination. A well-drafted multiple-choice question will usually have two choices that you can eliminate fairly easily and then you are left with two. Once you narrow your choices down to two, look to see which option best answers the question posed, even if they both sound right, there is only one right choice for multiple-choice questions.

Make sure you also read the directions for your multiple-choice section. Some schools use Scantron sheets for multiple-choice questions. If your law school has a time requirement for each portion of your exam, make sure you know whether you have to choose your answer *and* fill in your answers on the Scantron sheets in the time allotted. You do not want to spend the entire time working, thinking you will be given additional time to fill in the answers on the sheet, only to find out later that everything had to be completed within the time provided and now NONE of your answers will count (and yes, this has unfortunately has happened to a lot of students.) Additionally, make sure you allow enough time to go back and check your answers to make sure that your answer for each question correctly corresponds with the appropriate number on the Scantron sheet. With the amount of stress that you are under, it would be easy to simply skip a number, which will then affect the rest of your answers.

One key strategy for law school essay and multiple-choice exams is **PRACTICE, PRACTICE, PRACTICE.** The strategies discussed in this chapter will not benefit you if you do not have an opportunity to "try them out" before your actual exam. There are a number of sources you can use to find practice questions, starting with your professors. Also, your law school might have a "bank" of old exams or you can use commercial supplements that contain practice questions.

After the Exam

Once your exam ends do not "debrief" with other students. By this, I mean do not discuss what you thought the answers were with your classmates. If you get involved with discussing the test afterwards, you will likely find the following: (1) there will be at least one person who is absolutely certain that his/her answer was correct, (2) this answer will be different from yours, and (3) you will begin to doubt yourself and feel worse after the debriefing. You cannot change your answers once they are on the page so let it go and move on. My best advice to you is to go home, relax, and then prepare for your next exam.

"The difference between the impossible and the possible lies in a person's determination."

-Tommy Lasorda

Chapter 8

Seeking Help in Law School

Where To Go for Help

If you attend a law school that gives mid-terms for first year students, your mid-term grade will allow you to assess how well you have learned and can apply the information. For the rest of you, whose grade will be based on one final exam at the end of the semester, the question is, "How do you even know when you need help?" There is no such thing as getting too much help. There are several resources available to law students who need assistance with a particular class or concept. My recommendation is to use as many of the resources that your law school or law library provides to assist you with your studies. The following are some helpful resources if you need extra help in law school:

Peer Tutoring

Many law schools provide tutors who give weekly tutoring sessions for first year courses. These tutors are second-or third-year students who earned an "A" in that particular class. Tutoring sessions are usually done in large groups (rather than one-on-one peer tutoring) and are used to review material, answer questions, provide practice multiple-choice and essay questions and to assist you with any problems you may be having in the class. Most tutors work closely with the class professor to ensure that the information you receive is directly related to what is being discussed in class. Although some schools try to hire tutors that had the same professor of the students they are tutoring, this is not always an option as professors for 1L classes vary from year to year.

Academic Support

When I was in law school (now I really sound like my parents when they recounted their good ole' days), we did not have an

Academic Support Office. However, most law schools now have an office dedicated to providing curriculum support to its students. This office consists of law school graduates, whose sole job is to provide as much assistance to students as possible. If your law school provides this resource, the Academic Support Office will be an invaluable tool. Although its function varies depending on the school, the Academic Support Team typically conducts workshops for students, meets with students to assist them with any issues or problems they are having in class, provides a library of supplementary course materials to students and coordinates tutoring, mock exams and other programs. Make it a point during your first week of law school to find out where the Academic Support Office is and the forum(s) the office uses to advertise its programs and other opportunities for enrichment. You do not want to miss out on an opportunity because you didn't know about it. If your school does not have a designated Academic Support Office, find out which office at your law school sponsors opportunities for learning assistance. You may not have to use them, but it is good to know where and who to turn to when you do.

Supplementary Materials

Although canned briefs and commercial outlines tend to summarize the material from your casebooks, some supplementary materials, called hornbooks,[29] provide additional information and explanations of specific subjects. These books can be extremely helpful if you are having difficulty with a specific question or concept in class. Because these materials are exhaustive explanations of specific subjects, you should not read these books from cover to cover. Instead, you should use them as needed to help you to grasp a particular concept or to reinforce your learning if you are unsure about a specific area.

Professors

Although I will admit that I was too intimidated in law school to directly ask assistance from my professors, I would often pass by their offices and see fellow classmates there seeking additional help. Even, now, as I pass by other professors' offices, students are lined up at

---

[29] Hornbooks are "books explaining the basics of a given subject." Black's Law Dictionary at page 754.

their doors to see them. Professors now have regular office hours posted on their doors along with email addresses so students can contact them in the event they need additional assistance. One professor even posted her cell phone number on her door in the event that students need to speak with her outside of the posted office hours.

While most professors maintain an open door policy for students, it is important to understand that professors want to see that you have attempted to seek out the answer first through other resources. One year in my legal writing class, I met with students to review an outline they were required to turn in during their conference. One student, who clearly was not prepared with an outline, chose to meet with me anyway and instead of discussing the problem (which he had not begun to research yet), he wanted to discuss the issues that other students were having during their research. I do not know whether he thought it was a clever tactic or whether he was just grasping at straws, but needless to say, he failed to get any information from me other than some advice on being prepared and not procrastinating. Remember, professors know when you have done the work or want them to do it for you. They will not simply give you the information (mainly because the professor is testing you on the *analysis* and not necessarily the conclusion). Be prepared to work through the answer with them.

I will also caution you against being argumentative with your professor. I am still amazed by those who make it their purpose in law school to prove that they are smarter than the professor. Each year, there is at least one student (and if your class is divided into sections, undoubtedly there will be one in each section), who consistently challenges each professor in class. These students waste valuable class time (and inevitably valuable office time) arguing with the professor about why the case law was incorrectly decided or why the answer or explanation that the professor gave was wrong. If you think that the professor has made an error in class, respectively ask for clarification in class, discuss it privately with the professor during office hours or ask for clarification by email. It does not benefit you to try to belittle a professor. Most of these professors have been teaching this course for years and know their law, and even in one of the rare events that they have misspoken or misstated information in class, you will lose far more in the long run by trying to use that to elevate your own self-worth. Also, remember it is important to establish a good relationship with your professors as you might need them to serve as a reference or write a recommendation letter for you in the future.

Counseling Services

Some law schools, recognizing that law school is not just about your academic welfare but also your emotional welfare, now offer counseling services to students who may be experiencing emotional strains. If unresolved, these issues, which are sometimes a result of the stress that results from such an intense environment, will lead to even bigger emotional and academic problems. If you are experiencing problems in adjusting to the rigors of law school, do not be afraid to seek counseling. A counselor may be able to assist you in dealing with those emotional issues before they interfere with your academic success.

Learning Disabilities/Special Accommodations

Some students may require additional assistance in law school due to learning and/or other disabilities. If you have been previously diagnosed with a disability, contact the law school liaison to ensure that you receive appropriate accommodations. If you think that you have a disability that has not been diagnosed, arrange for testing as soon as possible, so as not to hinder your academic performance.

Additional Resources

If after exhausting all of the above resources you are still having difficulties, schedule an appointment with the Dean of Students at the law school to talk with him/her about your problems. The Dean of Students will be able to guide you and assist you in finding other solutions and resources. Make sure you come to the meeting with what you have done thus far to try to find a solution to your problems. Like your professors, the Dean of Students will not just provide you with an answer, but rather will assist you in finding the solution to your problems. Questions that the dean will ask are, "Are you doing everything you can to succeed?" "Are you devoting enough time to studying?" "Are there outside influences/issues preventing you from succeeding?" If you have not first exhausted all other resources, the dean is sure to first recommend that you do so before being able to assist you.

Whatever you do, do not give up. If it is truly your dream of becoming an attorney, keep working hard and stick with it. As I mentioned in Chapter 4, your first year is the most difficult year of law school. Although the second and third years will not be walks in the park, if you can get through this first year, you are well on your way to reaching graduation and passing the bar.

"Success in anything seems to be connected with action. Successful people keep moving. They make mistakes but they don't quit."

-Conrad Hilton

Chapter 9

Second Semester and Beyond

After Your First Semester

After you finish your first semester and enjoy a brief holiday break, you head back to tackle your second semester. Most of you have already received your grades and others will get them soon after you return for the spring semester. Whether you earned A's, B's, C's, or below, this chapter is about refocusing and regrouping so you can improve your performance in your second semester.

Refocusing and Regrouping

First, before you start your second semester, you should review your first semester and determine what worked for you, what did not work and what should be abandoned all together. Many students find that they perform better during second semester because the fear of the "unknown" from first semester has passed and that barrier is no longer in the way. However, for some people, it takes more than eliminating the fear. The following is a list of some common mistakes that need to be corrected for a successful second semester: (1) failing to attend classes regularly; (2) spending too much (or too little) time briefing cases; (3) spending too much (or too little) time preparing an outline/flashcards; (4) failing to find out how you would be tested; (5) failing to practice old exams; (6) failing to use all academic resources available; and (7) believing that serious financial, family problems or illnesses would not impact your learning.

If you were the student who did not think regular class attendance was important and your grades suffered because of it, then this is an easy fix. Go to class! The ABA mandates that every accredited law school require "regular and punctual class attendance."[30] Even if you did not regularly attend class as an undergraduate, you should operate

---

[30] American Bar Association 2009-2010 Standards 304(d).

on a different level in law school. There is no substitute for getting the information firsthand from your professor and classmates, even if you are best friends with the best note-taker in class. Although many law schools today record classes for student review, this should be used to clarify any areas you may have missed and not in lieu of attending class. So, unless you are seriously ill or another emergency arises, go to class regularly this semester and you should notice an improvement in your academic performance.

By this time, you should feel more comfortable with the essentials of law school – reading, briefing, outlining - and second semester will be more of the same. If you struggled with one or all of these skills during your first semester, now is the time to regroup. If reading and briefing was your problem first semester, revisit Chapter 4. Remember, you are reading the cases so you will be prepared for class discussion. You are not going to be tested on the facts and holdings of the cases. Also, it is likely that the previously unfamiliar legal terms are becoming a part of your vocabulary, so you do not have to spend as much time translating the words from legalese to plain English. With respect to briefing, at this point in the school year you should know what each professor focuses on when you discuss the assigned cases and your brief can be tailored to fit the class. Your class briefs are not for a grade, so stop trying to make them perfect. As long as your briefs help you follow along and participate in class discussions, then you are doing enough. However, once again, you do not want to fall into the trap of using commercial or "canned" briefs as a substitute for your own work. They may supply you with the basic information, but that particular editor's interpretation may not be what your professor is looking for in class. (Remember, the professor can tell which students use this shortcut.) Finally, keep in mind that certain cases will take longer to brief than others, but this is a skill where the more you do it, the less time it will take you to complete.

Did you try to make outlines or flash cards your first semester to learn the substantive law but it did not work for you? Again, this is where you have to be honest with yourself and assess if you used these methods properly. The key is to create your own personal study guide. Try alternate methods until you find one that works (flow charts, mind maps, or mnemonics). Remember to use the method that works best with your particular learning style. You cannot wait until the end of the semester to start compiling your study materials. I found that one of my problems in law school was procrastination; this is your worst enemy when it comes to creating outlines. I quickly learned that I needed to update my outlines regularly and save time to study from them. The same principle applies for flash cards, in that it will take you a considerable amount of time to prepare them, but they will be of no use to you if you do not have time to study them. If you developed a dependence on commercial outlines or outlines from other students and you used them to the exclusion of creating your own, just say "no." Commercial study aids are helpful but you do not want to supplant your ability to think like a lawyer with someone else's who has already graduated from law school. While you may find the answers, you will not be involved in the process required to get to the answer, which is the most important skill to have when you are taking exams.

Now you may have been the student who attended class regularly, spent a sufficient amount of time reading and briefing cases and properly outlined your material, but you still underperformed on your exams. Why? Well, possibly because you fall into the category of students who worked hard to learn the rules of law but did not spend enough time testing your ability to apply the law. You were the student who could recite all of the legal theories from your torts class but you never saw an essay question drafted by your torts professor prior to the actual exam. You were probably shocked when you sat down in your seat on exam day. You can reduce the chance of being surprised on exam day by asking the professor in advance about the format of the exam. Your exam preparation would not be complete without finding out how your professor is going to test you – whether she is giving you an essay exam, multiple-choice, short-answer or all of the above. Furthermore, you should seek as many opportunities as possible to work on practice questions prepared by professors in your law school.

If you completed an entire semester without setting foot into your Academic Support Office, do not make that same mistake this semester. There are many resources available to you at your law school and you should take advantage of them all. Introduce yourself to the academic support staff and make an appointment so you can establish a working relationship that will assist you throughout your law school career.

Challenges Outside of Law School

Of all the common mistakes that students make during their first semester, this last one is the one that you have the least control of, but it is the one that has the greatest potential to negatively impact your studies. Despite how bad you may want to, you cannot put life on hold while you adjust to one of the most difficult and rigorous academic experiences many of you have ever faced. So as life goes on, problems inevitably will arise and some can be managed without interruption to your studies, while others will disrupt you and prevent you from giving law school the attention it deserves. By no means am I suggesting that every cold or even a bout of the flu is cause to withdraw from law school because you missed a few classes. However, if you have to miss class for a substantial amount of time to handle a personal or medical emergency for yourself or a close family member, consider requesting a leave of absence and return to school when you have resolved your major life issues.

Do not be discouraged if your grades were not up to your expectations after the first semester. It is not too late and if you take a little time to regroup and refocus, you should see improvement. Make an appointment with your professors to review your fall semester exams (and no, this is not your opportunity to argue for a grade change), so you can figure out what you were missing. Make it your goal not to repeat the same mistakes from first semester. If you are willing to work consistently and if you are willing to make changes then you can have a more satisfying experience your second semester of law school and beyond.

"Success is the sum of small efforts, repeated day in and day out."

-Robert Collier

Chapter 10

Electives and Extracurricular Opportunities

Additional Considerations for Your First Year

While it is not possible for me to mention every aspect of your first year of law school in this book, I would be remiss if I didn't discuss some important things to consider in addition to your rigorous academic schedule.

Clubs and Organizations

You will have many opportunities to be involved in various aspects of student life in your first year of law school. The Student Bar Association, Phi Alpha Delta and the Student Division of the ACLU are just a few of the numerous organizations within law schools. In addition, there are class officer positions to fill and organizations to join that are specific to your law school and geared towards various areas of law and practice. Although the organizations will differ depending on the law school, my advice is the same: be careful not to become too involved in clubs and organizations your first year, especially your first semester.

Certainly, involvement in clubs and activities will enhance your resume. However, until you have established a solid foundation *and* effectively demonstrated your ability to balance school work with other activities, try to limit your involvement. This does not mean that you cannot attend meetings; just do not become so involved that it interferes with the purpose of your being there in the first place. When I was in law school, several of the students that were deeply involved in student government received grades that reflected their misplaced priorities (and were even in jeopardy of not graduating). Remember, potential employers will be looking at your first semester grades when hiring for summer internships. The internship after your first year could possibly lead to another internship after your second year and a job offer after you graduate and pass the bar. Once you have established a solid grade point average, you can then increase your involvement in these groups.

Moot Court, Trial Advocacy and Other Competitions

Law school will provide you with numerous opportunities to be involved in school-wide, state and national competitions. Teams, such as Trial Advocacy, which allows students to gain valuable skills and training in trial and litigation techniques; Moot Court, which provides students with opportunities to enhance appellate advocacy skills; and Client Counseling, in which students practice client interviews, are always recruiting students to represent the school in the various competitions. Additionally, your school may have other competitions designed for specific classes, which recognize students who excel in certain skills (such as presenting opening or closing arguments or legal writing competitions).

If you are interested in any of these competitions, first determine how much of a time commitment is required. Some competitions and schools, because of the demand on students' time and studies, limit participation to upper level students. If your school allows first-year students to participate in competitions the first year, make sure that you have a full understanding of the amount of time you will need to spend preparing for the competitions before getting involved. In addition to missing some classes, you may need to spend several hours a week (and as the competition approaches, several times a week) practicing. These are valuable ways to be involved in law school (I thoroughly enjoyed being involved in trial advocacy and opening argument competitions), but ensure that you can afford the time investment and allot for the time in your weekly schedule.

Selecting Courses for Second and Third Year

Since your courses will be predetermined for your first and second semester of law school, you will not be able to choose your own course load until your second and third year (a portion of your classes in second year will probably also be predetermined as well). It is not too early to start talking about selecting upper level courses.

Most schools have required courses and "highly" or "strongly" recommended courses." If you are planning to take the bar exam, make sure that you take all courses which will be tested on the bar exam, whether they are required or not. If you are interested in practicing in a specific area of law, select a course that will allow you to learn more about that topic or even provide you with practical skills that will assist you in your legal career. Be careful not to limit your electives to one area as it might hurt you if you later change your mind about the area of law you want to practice in, or if a prospective employer is interested in hiring someone who is familiar with various types of law rather that one specific area.

One final note about course selection: you will most certainly be given advice from other students on which professors give the most A's and/or which classes are the "easiest." It will be tempting to take courses to boost your grade point average or to take an "easy" course to balance out another difficult course. I was completely taken aback one day when one of my students approached me about receiving a B in my class. "I've never gotten any thing lower than an A in an elective course," she lamented. As the professor who taught the course the previous semester was known for not giving out much work and giving everyone good grades, the students constantly complained about the how hard the work (and my grading) was. Again, choose courses based on the benefit that it will provide to you in taking the bar and furthering your legal career. It may mean you have to work harder to get that A, but it will be more valuable to you in the long run.

Clinics

After your first year, you may want to take clinical classes. This is where you put your knowledge of the law into practice. Students involved in law school clinics will learn how to apply theoretical concepts to real-life legal situations. Most clinical courses have prerequisites so you will not be able to participate in the program during your first year, but you should speak to the clinical faculty now to find out what options are available at your school. Clinical programs have expanded from the basic civil and criminal litigation clinics to juvenile law, elder law, domestic violence law, small business law, immigration law and more. Clinical courses provide benefits to both you, as a student, and the local community that your law school serves. These opportunities enrich your law school experience and are worth considering when you select electives.

Law Review

Law Review is a student published academic journal that contains articles on various areas of the law. Most law schools have at least one primary law journal and a number of secondary journals. Law Review is another extracurricular activity that you may participate in during law school. You may become a part of your school's law review in two ways. One, you may "grade on" law review as a rising second year student if your GPA is high enough. Even if you do not grade on, you may have an opportunity to "write on" by participating in a writing competition during the summer after your first year. Most employers consider it a bonus for a student to participate on law review during their second year and an even greater bonus if the student is on the editorial board as a third-year student.

If you are interested in writing and research and would like to be a part of your school's law review, contact a current member of law review during your first year to find out more about law review. Also, your library should have back issues of not only your school's journals, but those of other law schools as well. Additionally, many law journals are available online. Do your research to determine if Law Review is an activity you would like to be involved with after your first year.

Summer Employment

The options for summer employment for law students are varied. However, as a first-year law student, you will be competing against second-year students for paid summer positions at law firms. Do not despair; this is when you need to be flexible and creative. If you are in a financial position to do so, volunteer your time at a law firm or government agency instead of seeking a paid position. You will open yourself up for more job opportunities in the tight job market.

You should also consider employment in a different city from where you attend school (maybe even your home town). If you attend law school in a major city, those markets are sometimes saturated by your fellow classmates and possibly by students from nearby law schools. However, rural areas or smaller cities and towns further away from your law school may have job vacancies. Several years ago I worked for an employer who had a difficult time finding a summer intern because our office was located approximately ninety minutes from the nearest law school. We sent job announcements to all the law schools and I personally contacted students that I knew to inform them about the job but most responded that the job was too far away (and this was a paid position.)

Utilize the Career Services Office in your law school for leads on summer employment opportunities. Interviews are often held on campus for summer internships, so make sure you have regular contact with Career Services to stay informed of all the latest summer internship postings. Finally, when you are looking for summer employment, make sure you look beyond the typical law firm job. There are positions for law students with federal, state and local governments, corporations, associations and perhaps even your own law school as a research assistant for one of your professors. Wherever you work after your first year, paid or unpaid, large firm or the legal department of a corporation, make sure that you gain as much experience as possible and use the experience to assist you in determining what type of law you want to practice after you graduate.

Summer School/Study Abroad

Some of you may not be able to find a summer job after your first year no matter how flexible and creative you are, so you should use the time to take summer courses at your law school or at another school for which your school allows you to transfer the credits. If you choose to attend summer school, you will likely find smaller classes and more opportunities to interact with your professors. However, the pace of summer school is faster than the semester and you will still need to manage your time and work hard (even when you are tempted by the pool or beach). One benefit of taking summer classes is that you can take a reduced course load in a later semester (perhaps to take on an externship) or you may even be interested in graduating early.

If you are interested in traveling to another country during the summer, you may want to look into programs which allow you to study abroad. Many law schools now offer their students the opportunity to earn credits while immersed in a foreign culture. Most study abroad programs teach international law or comparative law. In some cases, you will need to speak the foreign language of the country you are traveling to. If your school does not have a program, you still may be able to study abroad with another law school's program. Contact your Dean of Students or person who is responsible for international programs to find out important deadlines for applying to a program, as well as requesting additional financial aid if you are eligible.

These are only a few of the many considerations regarding law school after your first year. As I mentioned before, it is not possible to cover every aspect of law school in one book. The most important thing to remember is that by establishing a diligent work ethic and a solid foundation in law school your *first* year, you will position yourself to do well in your second and third year. First, once you have developed good study habits, these habits will follow you throughout law school (and when you take the bar exam). Second, your hard work will result in numerous opportunities within law school and after you graduate.

FINAL THOUGHTS FROM THE AUTHORS

"When you feel like giving up, remember why you held on for so long in the first place."

-Unknown

I ate, drank and slept law school during my first year. I did not have a life outside of studying. In the beginning, I admit that I let law school control my life. Even now, my husband likes to remind me of the statement he claims I made during one frantic weekend of studying, "law school was first and everything else, including him, was second." I have no recollection of this, but I might have said something along those lines as I was knee deep in contracts flash cards. I was extremely stressed and I questioned my own sanity for choosing such a difficult endeavor. By the end of my first year, I still considered dropping out of law school. Medical school looked better with every passing day. But, like I said before, I did not give up and I returned for my second and third years.

I encountered minor bumps during my first year like problems with my financial aid and the uninhabitable conditions of my apartment. I remember borrowing casebooks from my classmates in between classes and reading while everyone else was eating lunch because I did not have any money to buy my own books. I begrudgingly used credit cards to buy books and supplies until I received my financial aid check. I used the advocacy skills that I was developing in law school to advocate on my own behalf with the property managers of my apartment complex. But despite all of the issues I had to deal with outside of law school, I knew that I could not let them make me lose my focus. I had no excuse for not doing well because I did not have any major life disruptions and illnesses like my co-author and good friend. Seeing her continue in law school, despite her challenges, made me realize that I had no room to complain. Thankfully, my hard work netted positive results. I made Dean's List and I earned a scholarship because of my grades, which covered the cost of my tuition.

In my current position as Director of Academic Support, I advise many students on the skills that are necessary for law school success. Many of the strategies that I advise the students to use are the same strategies that I used when I was in law school (Okay, I listened to cassette tapes in my car, not CDs or mp3 files.) I am always pleased when a student returns to my office after they receive their grades and they see an improvement because they have utilized the strategies I shared with them. No one would ever say that law school is easy but it does not have to be an overwhelming experience. Let go of the anxiety, make sure you are always prepared, maintain balance in your school and personal life and do not be afraid to ask for help. I hope you take advantage of this book and use it to make your first year of law school a successful experience.

-KC

"It isn't sufficient just to want; you've got to ask yourself what you are going to do to get the things you want."

-Franklin D. Roosevelt

Each year, as finals near, my first-year students always ask me to give them one piece of advice to help them do well on their exams. My answer to them is always the same: "If I could do it, then so can you." This response is usually followed by moans and groans from students who expected to find out the secret, or rather the shortcut, that would enable them to do well with the least investment. Although I always refuse to alter my answer, I do, however share with them my story that I hope will serve to encourage them and motivate them to do well. And so now, in my "final words" I want to share my story with you.

My first year, which I now look back on with much amusement, was fraught with- as my kids would say-"drama." It started off with my dad being diagnosed with prostrate cancer and having surgery to remove it during the first couple of weeks of school. The next problem arose during the end of the first semester when I had my own medical emergency and I was rushed to the hospital with a blood clot in my leg. I laugh now when I remember the doctor telling me that I had to be admitted to the hospital for ten-yes, TEN days- and telling him that I was in law school and that missing ten days of class was simply not going to happen. Although he thought I was crazy for doing so (and now so do I), he instead kept me for only the weekend and I had to go to the hospital every morning for the next week to do a blood draw to check my levels and then inject myself in the stomach according to the results of my blood test on that morning. And as if that were not enough, I started losing my hearing and, for a short period was completely deaf, with no accommodations available to me. Since the loss happened so quickly I had no opportunity to learn sign language. Oh, and did I mention I was planning my wedding which took place the summer after my first year? So... when I say to you, if I could do it, so can you, I mean it from the bottom of my heart. There was no easy way to do it, nor was there a magic button to press to make law school easier. I received no preferential treatment and had to learn by copying the notes of my study partner (and now one of my closest friends and co-author of this book) each day as she took them in class. While it was not easy and I wanted to really feel sorry for myself and give up, I was fortunate to have people around me telling me what I now tell to you: "Do not give up." Whatever happens your first year, if this is something you want to do, continue to work hard and it will all come together. I not only graduated, but graduated with honors, so I if I could do it, I know you WILL too! Best of luck as you embark on this incredible and memorable journey.

-KV